Original edition published in English under the title *Words of Thanks* by Lion Publishing, Tring, England, copyright © 1974 Lion Publishing.

First published in the United States and Canada in 1983 by Thomas Nelson Publishers.

Published in Nashville, Tennessee, by Thomas Nelson, Inc. and distributed in Canada by Lawson Falle, Ltd., Cambridge, Ontario.

Photographs by Lion Publishing/David Alexander.

Scripture quotations are from the *Good News Bible*—Old Testament: Copyright © American Bible Society 1976; New Testament: Copyright © American Bible Society 1966, 1971, 1976.

ISBN 0-8407-5342-X

—Words of—
THANKS

Thomas Nelson Publishers
Nashville • Camden • New York

THANK YOU, LORD

I thank you, Lord, with all my heart;
I sing praise to you before the gods.
I face your holy Temple, bow down,
and praise your name
because of your constant love and faithfulness,
because you have shown that your name and
your commands are supreme.
You answered me when I called to you;
with your strength you strengthened me.

All the kings in the world will praise you, Lord,
because they have heard your promises.
They will sing about what you have done,
and about your great glory.
Even though you are so high above,
you care for the lowly,
and the proud cannot hide from you.

PSALM 138:1–6

In the village of Bethany, Jesus stayed in the humble home of
Martha, Mary and Lazarus.

FAITHFUL AND JUST

Praise the Lord!

With all my heart I will thank the Lord
in the assembly of his people.
How wonderful are the things the Lord does!
All who are delighted with them want to
understand them.
All he does is full of honor and majesty;
his righteousness is eternal . . .

In all he does he is faithful and just;
all his commands are dependable.
They last for all time;
they were given in truth and righteousness.
He set his people free
and made an eternal covenant with them.
Holy and mighty is he!
The way to become wise is to have reverence for
the Lord;
he gives sound judgment to all who obey his
commands.
He is to be praised forever.

PSALM 111:1–3, 7–10

The sun sets over a landscape in central Turkey.

AS LONG AS I LIVE

Praise the Lord!
Praise the Lord, my soul!
I will praise him as long as I live;
I will sing to my God all my life.

Don't put your trust in human leaders,
no human being can save you.
When they die, they return to the dust;
on that day all their plans come to an end . . .

The Lord sets prisoners free
and gives sight to the blind.
He lifts those who have fallen;
he loves his righteous people.
He protects the strangers who live in our land;
he helps widows and orphans,
but ruins the plans of the wicked . . .

The Lord is king forever.
Your God, O Zion, will reign for all time.

Praise the Lord!

PSALM 146:1–4, 8–10

Two girls look after the flock of sheep and goats near
Beersheba, Israel.

HE GIVES ANIMALS THEIR FOOD . . .

Praise the Lord!

It is good to sing praise to our God;
it is pleasant and right to praise him . . .

He has decided the number of the stars
and calls each one by name.
Great and mighty is our Lord;
his wisdom cannot be measured.
He raises the humble,
but crushes the wicked to the ground.
Sing hymns of praise to the Lord;
play music on the harp to our God.
He spreads clouds over the sky;
he provides rain for the earth
and makes grass grow on the hills.
He gives animals their food
and feeds the young ravens when they call . . .

He takes pleasure in those who honor him,
in those who trust in his constant love . . .

Praise the Lord!

PSALM 147:1, 4–9, 11, 20

Cattle seek pasture among the rocks of Galilee.

MY SAVIOR

How I love you, Lord!
You are my defender.
The Lord is my protector;
he is my strong fortress.
My God is my protection,
and with him I am safe.
He protects me like a shield;
he defends me and keeps me safe.
I call to the Lord,
and he saves me from my enemies.
Praise the Lord!

PSALM 18:1–3

The great walls and gates of the old city of Jerusalem.

14

GOD'S FLOCK

Come, let us praise the Lord!
Let us sing for joy to God, who protects us!
Let us come before him with thanksgiving
and sing joyful songs of praise.
For the Lord is a mighty God,
a mighty king over all the gods.
He rules over the whole earth,
from the deepest caves to the highest hills.
He rules over the sea, which he made;
the land also, which he himself formed.

Come, let us bow down and worship him;
let us kneel before the Lord, our Maker!
He is our God;
we are the people he cares for,
the flock for which he provides.

PSALM 95:1–7

A shepherd with his flocks beside the Lake of Galilee.

GOD HAS HELPED ME

Give praise to the Lord;
he has heard my cry for help.
The Lord protects and defends me;
I trust in him.
He gives me help and makes me glad;
I praise him with joyful songs.

The Lord protects his people;
he defends and saves his chosen king.
Save your people, Lord,
and bless those who are yours.
Be their shepherd,
and take care of them forever.

PSALM 28:6–9

A typical Middle Eastern street, with old and young.

THIRST WILL BE SATISFIED

O God, you are my God,
and I long for you.
My whole being desires you;
like a dry, worn-out, and waterless land,
my soul is thirsty for you.
Let me see you in the sanctuary;
let me see how mighty and glorious you are.
Your constant love is better than life itself,
and so I will praise you.
I will give you thanks as long as I live;
I will raise my hands to you in prayer.
My soul will feast and be satisfied,
and I will sing glad songs of praise to you.

PSALM 63:1–5

A goat satisfies its thirst from the fresh water of the Lake of
Galilee.

HOW GOOD THE LORD IS

I will always thank the Lord;
I will never stop praising him.
I will praise him for what he has done;
may all who are oppressed listen and be glad!
Proclaim with me the Lord's greatness;
let us praise his name together!

I prayed to the Lord, and he answered me;
he freed me from all my fears.
The oppressed look to him and are glad;
they will never be disappointed.
The helpless call to him, and he answers;
he saves them from all their troubles.
His angel guards those who have reverence for
the Lord and rescues them from danger.

Find out for yourself how good the Lord is.
Happy are those who find safety with him.
Have reverence for the Lord, all his people;
those who obey him have all they need.
Even lions go hungry for lack of food,
but those who obey the Lord lack nothing good.

PSALM 34:1-10

Two riders on a track through the Syrian desert pass an oasis
of green trees.

ALL NATIONS, ALL PEOPLES

Praise the Lord, all nations!
Praise him, all peoples!
His love for us is strong,
and his faithfulness is eternal.

Praise the Lord!

PSALM 117

Children play in the streets of the old city of Jerusalem.

24

GOD SAVES

I waited patiently for the Lord's help;
then he listened to me and heard my cry.
He pulled me out of a dangerous pit,
out of the deadly quicksand.
He set me safely on a rock
and made me secure.
He taught me to sing a new song,
a song of praise to our God.
Many who see this will take warning
and will put their trust in the Lord . . .

Lord, I know you will never stop being merciful
to me.
Your love and loyalty will always keep me safe.

PSALM 40:1–3, 11

Pits, or cisterns, were dug in ancient Israel to store water, or
to gain access to it.

GOD CARES

Praise the Lord!

You servants of the Lord,
praise his name!
His name will be praised,
now and forever!
From the east to the west
praise the name of the Lord!
The Lord rules over all nations;
his glory is above the heavens.

There is no one like the Lord our God.
He lives in the heights above,
but he bends down
to see the heavens and the earth.
He raises the poor from the dust;
he lifts the needy from their misery
and makes them companions of princes,
the princes of his people.
He honors the childless wife in her home;
he makes her happy by giving her children.

Praise the Lord!

PSALM 113

A woman in rural Syria goes about her daily tasks.

ALL LIVING THINGS

The Lord is faithful to his promises,
and everything he does is good.
He helps those who are in trouble;
he lifts those who have fallen.
All living things look hopefully to you,
and you give them food when they need it.
You give them enough
and satisfy the needs of all.
The Lord is righteous in all he does,
merciful in all his acts.
He is near to those who call to him,
who call to him with sincerity.
He supplies the needs of those who honor him;
he hears their cries and saves them.
He protects everyone who loves him,
but he will destroy the wicked.
I will always praise the Lord;
let all creatures praise his holy name forever.

PSALM 145:13–21

Storks are migrant visitors to Israel.

PRAISE THE LORD, MY SOUL!

Praise the Lord, my soul!
All my being, praise his holy name!
Praise the Lord, my soul,
and do not forget how kind he is.
He forgives all my sins
and heals all my diseases.
He keeps me from the grave
and blesses me with love and mercy.
He fills my life with good things,
so that I stay young and strong like an eagle . . .

The Lord placed his throne in heaven;
he is king over all.
Praise the Lord, you strong and mighty angels,
who obey his commands,
who listen to what he says.
Praise the Lord, all you heavenly powers,
you servants of his, who do his will!
Praise the Lord, all his creatures
in all the places he rules.
Praise the Lord, my soul!

PSALM 103:1–5, 19–22

Working the treadle of a traditional hand-loom in the old city
of Damascus.

HOW GREAT YOU ARE!

We give thanks, to you, O God, we give thanks
to you!
We proclaim how great you are
and tell of the wonderful things you have
done! . . .

Judgment does not come from the east or from
the west,
from the north or from the south;
it is God who is the judge,
condemning some and acquitting others.
The Lord holds a cup in his hand,
filled with the strong wine of his anger.
He pours it out, and all the wicked drink it;
they drink it down to the last drop.

But I will never stop speaking of the God of
Jacob
or singing praises to him.
He will break the power of the wicked,
but the power of the righteous will be increased.

PSALM 75:1, 6–10

Behind the thorns, the sparkle of light gleaming on water.

WHY AM I TROUBLED?

Send your light and your truth;
may they lead me
and bring me back to Zion, your sacred hill,
and to your Temple, where you live.
Then I will go to your altar, O God,
you are the source of my happiness.
I will play my harp and sing praise to you,
O God, my God.

Why am I so sad?
Why am I so troubled?
I will put my hope in God,
and once again I will praise him,
my savior and my God.

PSALM 43:3–5

Across the valley from the Temple area of Jerusalem, these
ancient olive-trees are in the Garden of Gethsemane.

THE GOD OF HISTORY

Give thanks to the Lord, proclaim his greatness,
tell the nations what he has done.
Sing praise to the Lord;
tell the wonderful things he has done.
Be glad that we belong to him;
let all who serve the Lord rejoice.
Go to the Lord for help;
and worship him continually.
You descendants of Abraham, his servant;
you descendants of Jacob, the man he chose:
remember the miracles that God performed
and the judgments that he gave.

Praise the Lord!

PSALM 105:1–6

The moon above the mountains of Sinai, where Israel
received the law from God.

THIS GOD IS OUR GOD

Inside your temple, O God,
we think of your constant love.
You are praised by people everywhere,
and your fame extends over all the earth.
You rule with justice;
let the people of Zion be glad!
You give right judgments;
let there be joy in the cities of Judah!
People of God, walk round Zion and count the
towers;
take notice of the walls and examine the
fortresses,
so that you may tell the next generation:
"This God is our God, forever and ever;
he will lead us for all time to come."

PSALM 48:9–14

The great south-eastern corner of the wall of the Temple area
of Jerusalem.

PRAISE HIM WITH HARPS

Praise the Lord!

Praise God in his Temple!
Praise his strength in heaven!
Praise him for the mighty things he has done.
Praise his supreme greatness.

Praise him with trumpets.
Praise him with harps and lyres.
Praise him with drums and dancing.
Praise him with harps and flutes.
Praise him with cymbals.
Praise him with loud cymbals.
Praise the Lord, all living creatures.

Praise the Lord!

PSALM 150

A reconstruction in the Music Museum, Haifa, of the type of
harp used by David.

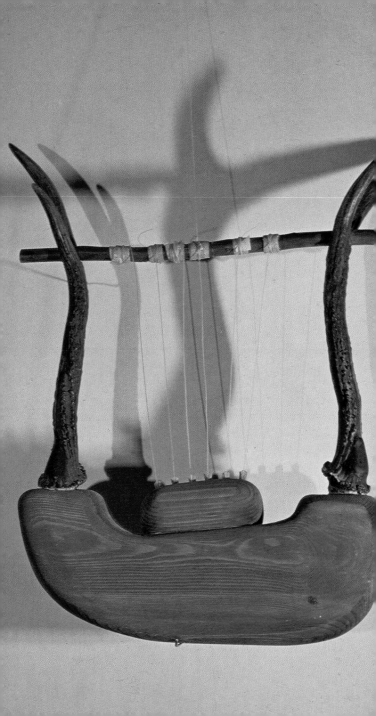

PRAISE HIM, ALL THAT HE HAS MADE

Praise the Lord!

Praise the Lord from heaven,
you that live in the heights above.
Praise him, all his angels,
all his heavenly armies.

Praise him, sun and moon;
praise him, shining stars.
Praise him, highest heavens,
and the waters above the sky . . .

Praise the Lord from the earth,
sea monsters and all ocean depths;
lightning and hail, snow and clouds,
strong winds that obey his command.

Praise him, hills and mountains,
fruit trees and forests;
all animals, tame and wild,
reptiles and birds.

Praise him, kings and all peoples,
princes and all other rulers;
girls and young men,
old people and children too.

Let them all praise the name of the Lord . . .

Praise the Lord!

PSALM 148:1–4, 7–13, 14

The sun sinks behind the cedars of Lebanon.